S0-BZM-970

GEOMETRY
AND
TRIGONOMETRY

GEOMETRY

AND

TRIGONOMETRY

EDITED BY JAMES STANKOWSKI

Britannica
Educational Publishing

IN ASSOCIATION WITH

ROSEN
EDUCATIONAL SERVICES

Published in 2015 by Britannica Educational Publishing (a trademark of Encyclopædia Britannica, Inc.) in association with The Rosen Publishing Group, Inc.
29 East 21st Street, New York, NY 10010

Distributed exclusively by Rosen Publishing.
To see additional Britannica Educational Publishing titles, go to rosenpublishing.com.

First Edition

Britannica Educational Publishing
J. E. Luebering: Director, Core Reference Group
Anthony L. Green: Editor, Compton's by Britannica

Rosen Publishing
Hope Lourie Killcoyne: Executive Editor
Kathy Campbell: Editor
Nelson Sá: Art Director
Brian Garvey: Designer
Cindy Reiman: Photography Manager

Introduction and supplementary material by John Strazzabosco

Library of Congress Cataloging-in-Publication Data

Geometry and trigonometry/edited by James Stankowski.—First edition.
         pages cm.—(The story of math, core principles of mathematics)
Includes bibliographical references and index.
ISBN 978-1-62275-527-1 (library bound)
1. Geometry. 2. Trigonometry. I. Stankowski, James, editor.
QA445.G474 2015
516—dc23
                                                                          2014018167
Manufactured in the United States of America

Contents

This book covers a broad collection of the principles of geometry and trigonometry inside a nice, compact format for the middle school and early high school student. Colorful diagrams bring the principles to life. The topics are enriched by references to famous mathematicians who discovered these principles and also snapshots of these principles at work in the real world. Seldom does a math book bring the story of so many topics in such a comprehensible way.

The student will find a wonderful resource that can always be consulted for quick help and location of ideas that arise even years later during formal math study and beyond.

Of course math discoveries are fascinating in themselves, and when they lead to wonderful, useful inventions, one sees why people study these ideas in the first place.

For instance, could a basic geometric shape be used to stop excruciating pain? Perhaps Euclid didn't have disease in mind when he began organizing the simplest of geometric figures, such as points, lines, and curves. But over the years other mathematicians took his shapes, and proved that certain geometric properties had qualities that today make people feel better, even if those individuals happen to be doubled over in pain from what are called kidney stones.

The particular geometrical shape required for medical healing in this case is called an ellipse, featured in this book. Inside the ellipse (or its three-dimensional relative, an egg shape or ellipsoid) is a point called a focus, near one end of the shape. Another focus appears near the other end of the shape. Scientists found

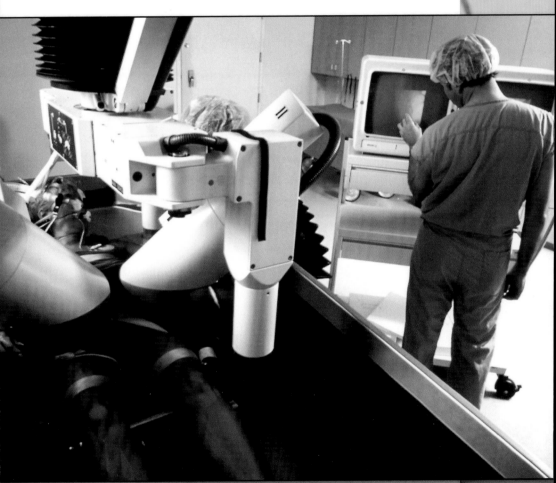

In lithotripsy, a lithotripter uses an ellipsoid and a focus point to send sound waves to shatter a patient's gallstones or kidney stones into miniscule pieces. Southern Illinois University/Photo Researchers/Getty Images

that shooting sonar waves from one focus makes sounds that bounce off the inside walls of the ellipsoid, and they *all* strike the other focus at once, like a gentle hammer.

That's how doctors use those sounds, special instruments (such as a lithotripter machine), and ellipsoids to help break up kidney stones in the patient. No surgery is needed. The patient makes a faster recovery than if surgery had been used. His or her kidney stones are painlessly shattered with no harm to the kidney, and the patient might go to school or work the very next day.

When readers enter the pages of this book and see the basics of geometry and trigonometry, it pays to ask themselves with each figure they see, could they discover some great invention with this shape? Could they save lives? Could they ease pain? Could they somehow use it to create a new invention? What problem might they solve with it?

Students will discover why trigonometry is called that, and they'll see a math topic begin to unfold that, strangely, they have already used quite a bit even though they might not have been aware of it. Trigonometry is embedded in the software of computers. When people have played a computer game where their car, for instance, spins and misses trouble on the road, the joystick is really telling the computer to use trigonometry formulas to get the car to do what the players want. So the math comes alive for these individuals. They'll encounter in this book some basics of trigonometry, often fondly called "trig."

Finally, readers will also find fascinating information on great mathematicians who made the ideas of geometry and trigonometry apply to wonderful discoveries that have changed the world they live in.

1

EUCLIDEAN GEOMETRY

The ancient branch of mathematics known as geometry deals with points, lines, surfaces, and solids—and their relationships. In particular, geometry may be thought of as offering (1) precise definitions of many different figures; (2) construction methods for drawing figures; (3) a wealth of facts about the figures; and, most important, (4) ways to prove the facts.

Geometry was thoroughly organized in about 300 BCE, when the Greek mathematician Euclid gathered what was known at the time, added original work of his own, and arranged 465 propositions into 13 books, collectively called *Elements*. The books covered not only plane and solid geometry but also much of what is now known as algebra, trigonometry, and advanced arithmetic.

Down through the ages, the propositions have been rearranged, and many of the proofs are different, but the basic idea presented in the *Elements* has not changed. In the work, facts are not just cataloged but are developed in an orderly way, starting with statements (definitions, common notions, and postulates) that seem perfectly self-evident, with each successive theorem proved by using only previously shown facts. This mode of reasoning, known as the axiomatic method, has profoundly influenced epistemology (the study of the nature, origin, and limits of human knowledge) and education.

Even in 300 BCE, geometry was recognized to be not just for mathematicians. Anyone can benefit from the basic teachings of geometry, which are how to follow lines of reasoning, how to say precisely what is intended, and especially how to prove basic concepts by following these lines of reasoning. Taking a course in geometry is beneficial for all students, who will find that learning to reason and prove convincingly is necessary for every profession. It is true that not everyone must prove things, but everyone is exposed to proof. Politicians, advertisers, and many other people try to offer convincing arguments. Anyone who cannot tell a good proof from a bad one may easily be persuaded in the wrong direction. Geometry

Euclid works with a compass (a tool used in drawing circles) in a 14th-centu[ry] marble panel on the Campanile (bell tower) of Santa Maria del Fiore [in] Florence, Italy. A. Dagli Orti/De Agostini Picture Library/Getty Images

EUCLID

It has been said that, next to the Bible, the *Elements* of Euclid is the most translated, published, and studied tome in the Western world. Of the author himself almost nothing is known. It is recorded that he founded and taught at a school of mathematics in Alexandria, Egypt, during the reign of Ptolemy I Soter, who ruled from 323 to about 283 BCE. It is assumed from his books that he was not a first-class mathematician, but he was a first-rate teacher of geometry and arithmetic. The *Elements* remained unchallenged for more than 2,000 years. Not until the mid-19th century was a non-Euclidean geometry devised.

To compile his *Elements* Euclid relied on the work of several predecessors, so the treatise is of uneven quality. Once it was published, the *Elements* superseded all previous mathematical treatises and became the standard text. During the Middle Ages three Arabic translations were made of the work, and it was through these that it became known in Europe. The English traveler and philosopher Adelard of Bath went to Spain disguised as a Muslim student and obtained an Arabic copy, from which he made a Latin translation in 1120. The first Latin translation of the Greek without an Arabic intermediary was made by Bartolomeo Zamberti and published in Venice in 1505. There have been several more recent translations into other languages. Among Euclid's other works on geometry were *Data* and *On Divisions*. He also wrote *Optics* and *The Elements of Music*. Some of his writings have been lost, while other works are wrongly credited to him.

provides a simplified universe, where points and lines obey believable rules and where conclusions are easily verified. By first studying how to reason in this simplified universe, people can eventually, through practice and experience, learn how to reason in a complicated world.

Geometry in ancient times was recognized as part of everyone's education. Early Greek philosophers asked that no one come to their schools who had not learned the *Elements* of Euclid. There were, and still are, many who resisted this kind of education. It is said that Ptolemy I asked Euclid for an easier way to learn the material. Euclid told him there was no "royal road" to geometry. The same message applies to readers today. They will not learn what geometry is all about. What they will learn is the basic shapes of some of the figures dealt with in geometry and a few facts about them. It takes a geometry course, with textbook and teacher, to show the complete and orderly arrangement of the facts and how each is proved.

POINTS, LINES, AND ANGLES

Geometric figures are based on points and lines. Euclid began his *Elements* with a series of definitions, starting with these two:

A point is that which has no part.

A line is breadthless length.

Because he had not explained the words "part," "breadth," or "length," he was not defining these figures in terms of simpler things. The fact is that points and lines are so simple that they cannot be defined perfectly, but other things can be defined in terms of them. Definitions in this volume will not be stated in full detail, as they would be in a geometry text-book, but they will be described briefly to show how they are linked, leading from points and lines to very special figures.

A line is usually drawn with arrowheads to show that it extends without end in both directions. A ray is half of a line—with just one endpoint. Two rays with the same endpoint form an angle. If the rays are the two halves

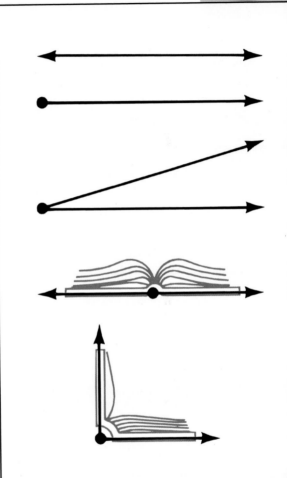

Some different geometric figures are (from top to bottom): a line, a ray, an angle, a straight angle, and a right angle. The latter two are also shown as an open book. Encyclopædia Britannica, Inc.

of the same line, the angle is a straight angle. For measuring purposes, a straight angle may be thought to be like a book opened flat on a desk. An angle opened half that far is a right angle; its sides are perpendicular to one another.

For smaller angular measurements, the right angle is divided into 90 equal parts, each part being one degree of arc; therefore, half a right angle is 45 degrees, written as 45°. Four right angles measure 360°.

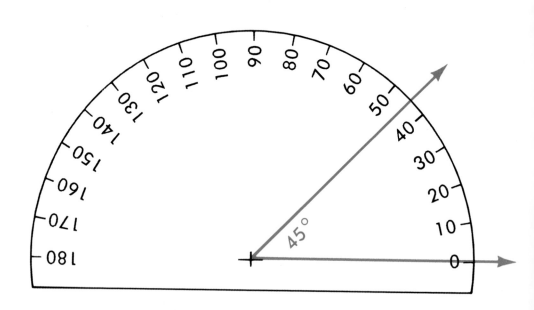

A 45° angle is half a right angle (90°) and a quarter of a straight angle (180°). Encyclopædia Britannica, Inc.

Any angle smaller than a right angle is acute; those larger than a right angle but smaller than a straight angle are obtuse. Any angle larger than a straight angle is said to be reflex. It has the same sides as an angle that is not reflex, but the angle is measured the long way around; there is certainly a difference between a book opened 340° and one opened 20°.

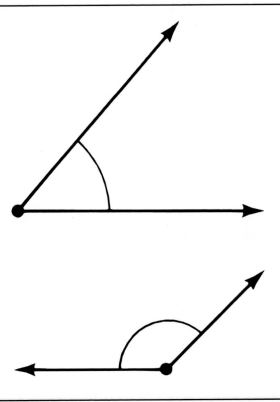

An acute angle (top) is smaller than a right angle, while an obtuse angle (bottom) is larger than a right angle but smaller than a straight angle. Encyclopædia Britannica, Inc.

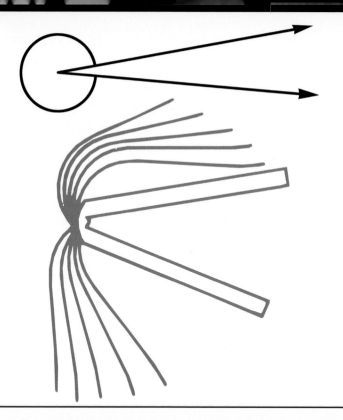

A reflex angle (top and bottom, as an open book) *is larger than a straight angle.* Encyclopædia Britannica, Inc.

CONSTRUCTION

In the illustrations for this discussion, points and lines have been shown in color, which has been helpful in showing relationships. These representations, however, are definitely not real-istic. Lines do not even have thickness, much less color. A picture that comes closer to a true representation is shown on page 19:

In the diagram, the border line between the red and white areas is neither red nor white, and it has no thickness; it is much like a true

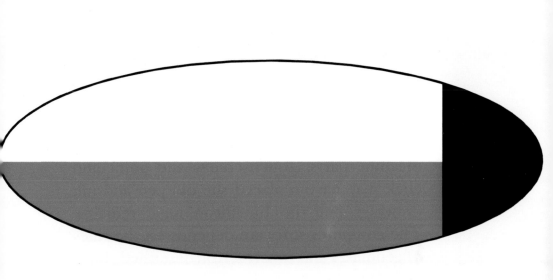

A diagram represents a line—the border between the red and white areas— and a point—the place where that line meets the black region. Encyclopædia Britannica, Inc.

line. The place where this line runs into the black region is much like a true point, with no dimensions at all. It is much more practical for everyday calculations to represent points by dots and to represent lines by paths of black or color. Nonetheless, the reasoning applied to the figures can be exact even if the diagrams are not.

Geometers and drafters use two instruments, an unmarked straightedge (for ruling lines, but not for measuring them) and a simple compass (for drawing circles of various sizes). These instruments are enough to do everything from copying a line segment to constructing a square with the same area as any given polygon.

Modern drafters employ computers to create drawings used to make machines and machine parts. Touchscreens and point and click may have replaced the old pen and ink drawings but the Euclidean logic remains. The computer software depends on the rules of geometry and construction described above and also rules that follow below.

PLANE FIGURES

The sides of an angle are unending rays, but the rays can be cut into segments without changing the opening between the rays, which is the means by which angles are measured. Segment lengths are important in the next chain description, which leads from lines to the most special kinds of triangles.

A line segment is part of a line, with two endpoints. A broken line is made up of line segments joined end to end; if the ends of the broken line meet, it is a closed broken-line, or polygon. A polygon with three sides is a triangle. If all three angles are acute, it is an acute triangle. If an acute triangle has two equal sides it is an acute-isosceles triangle. (Any isosceles triangle has two equal sides.) If all three sides of a triangle are equal, it is an equilateral triangle. There are other interesting kinds of triangles not described here, but every kind

TRIANGLES

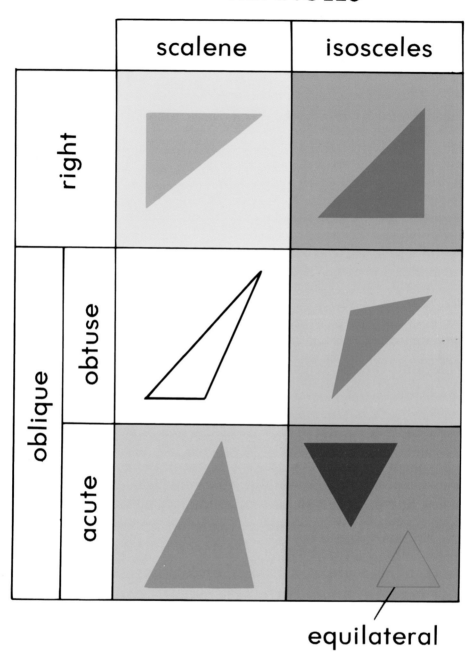

	scalene	isosceles
right		
oblique — **obtuse**		
oblique — **acute**		

equilateral

A chart shows the basic types of triangles. Encyclopædia Britannica, Inc.

will fit into one of the six categories shown on the chart on page 22. A triangle with one right angle is a right triangle. All obtuse triangles are oblique, but so are acute triangles. A scalene triangle has no equal sides. An equilateral triangle has three, but this does not disqualify it from being isosceles. Equilateral triangles form a subset of acute-isosceles triangles.

An excellent way of representing subsets and the like is the use of Venn diagrams. Each

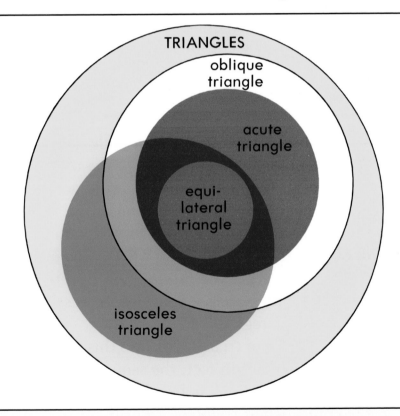

A Venn diagram represents the sets and subsets of different types of triangles. For example, the set of acute triangles contains the subset of equilateral triangles because all equilateral triangles are acute. Encyclopædia Britannica, Inc.

JOHN VENN

An English logician and philosopher, John Venn (1834–1923) is best known as the inventor of diagrams known as Venn diagrams. These are graphs that use overlapping curves and circles to show collections of mathematical elements and what they have in common. Venn attended the University of Cambridge in England and graduated with a degree in mathematics. He developed his diagramming method in *Symbolic Logic* (1881), a book that he wrote in defense of the English mathematician George Boole's attempt to represent logical relations in algebraic terms. In 1883, he became a member of the Royal Society, one of the oldest and most distinguished scientific societies in Great Britain, in recognition for his work in math and logic.

set or subset is represented by a circle or a blob of some other shape, as shown in the diagram on page 23. One circle shown inside another means that one set is contained in the other, as the set of acute triangles is shown within the set of oblique triangles. The area where two circles overlap represents the intersection of sets, as that for acute-isosceles triangles, represented by the purple region.

Every kind of triangle fits into this diagram somewhere. It is, in fact, the same diagram as the previous one, as can be seen by comparing the colors. Right triangles, though not named on this Venn diagram, are represented by the yellow and green regions.

The regions on a Venn diagram represent sets, often with unlimited numbers of elements, as in the case of triangles. The regions are not supposed to look like the members of the set themselves, but for polygons that have more sides than triangles, it is possible to have the shapes of the regions illustrate the figures themselves as well as to show how the sets are related. This is done on the diagram, which represents part of the vast set of polygons.

QUADRILATERALS

A polygon with four sides is a quadrilateral. Quadrilaterals exist in many more shapes than do triangles, but not all have special names. That is why the diagram shows some space inside "quadrilateral" in addition to that filled with specific kinds.

The kite is a shape not often mentioned in geometry books, but it is a familiar and interesting shape, with two pairs of adjacent equal sides. A parallelogram has both pairs of opposite sides parallel. If the same figure is both a kite and a parallelogram, it is an equilateral quadrilateral, or a rhombus. Another special kind of parallelogram is the rectangle, with four right angles. A square, with four right angles and all sides equal, is a special kind of rectangle, rhombus, kite, and parallelogram.

Another family of quadrilaterals is the trapezoids, which have one pair of parallel sides. It might be thought that a parallelogram is a special example of a trapezoid, just as an equilateral triangle is a special example of an isosceles triangle. But in this case it works out better to specify that a trapezoid has only two parallel sides. If the other two sides are equal, it is an isosceles trapezoid; if it has right angles at one end, it is a right trapezoid. But there can be no right-isosceles trapezoids; if a trapezoid were both right and isosceles it would be a rectangle. It would then have another pair of parallel sides and be completely disqualified from being a trapezoid.

People see the many kinds of quadrilaterals more often than they realize. Squares that appear in man-made forms and in the natural world, however, are not usually seen as squares. The diagram on page 28, for example, that shows a perspective view of a cubical room, contains a square doorway, a square window, and a square rug. The view is a realistic one, such as a camera would make, and it shows the doorway as an isosceles trapezoid, the window as a right trapezoid, and the floor as a kite. The walls appear as trapezoids that are neither right nor isosceles, and the rug is no special kind of quadrilateral at all. The picture of the dice

POLYGONS

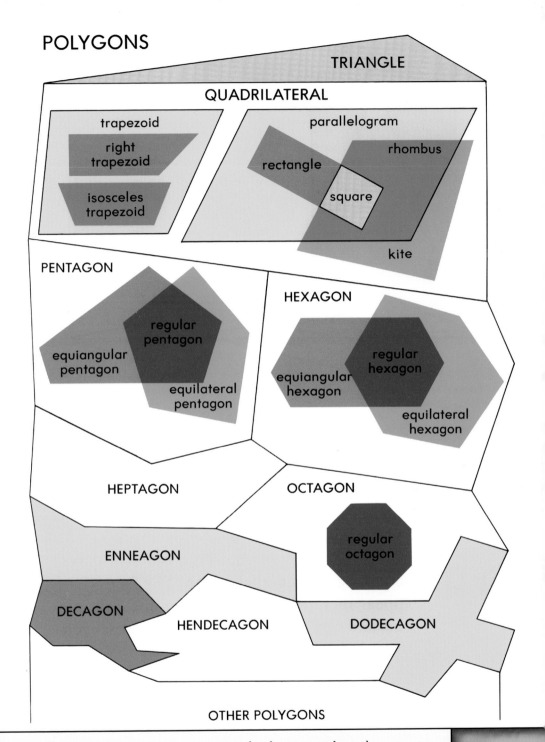

A Venn diagram represents certain sets of polygons, with each region in the form of the polygon it represents. Encyclopædia Britannica, Inc.

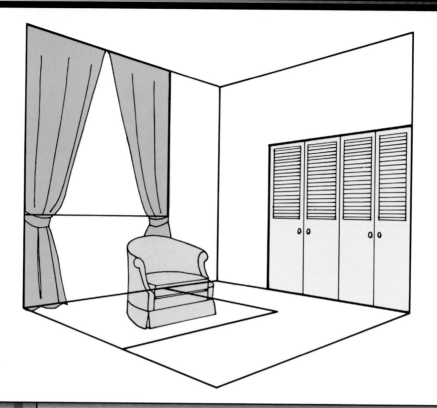

A perspective view of a cubical room shows a room with a square doorway, square window, and a square rug. Encyclopædia Britannica, Inc.

in the second diagram on page 29 is another kind of view of squares, not quite so realistic as the view of the room but still quite close to what is actually seen. The faces that appear include two parallelograms, a rhombus, and two rectangles but no squares, even though the faces of dice are square.

OTHER POLYGONS

Pentagons, with five corners, and hexagons, with six, can take on even more shapes than

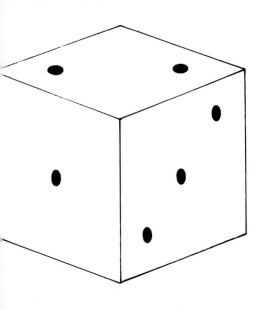

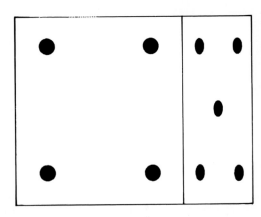

Although all the faces of a pair of dice are square, the faces appear in this view as two parallelograms, a rhombus, and two rectangles. *Encyclopædia Britannica, Inc.*

quadrilaterals; named kinds of pentagons and hexagons are even scarcer than named kinds of quadrilaterals. Three common adjectives applied to polygons of more than four sides are equilateral, having all sides equal; equiangular, having all angles equal; and regular, both equilateral and equiangular. These are shown in the polygon chart for pentagons and hexagons (see page 27).

The names equilateral, equiangular, and regular are not usually used with quadrilateral. In the case of triangles, every equilateral triangle is also equiangular and, therefore, regular.

The heptagon has seven corners, and the octagon has eight. The enneagon, nine corners, is sometimes called a nonagon. The other prefixes used are the Greek names for numbers, but nona- is Latin. Other Latin names, however, are quadrilateral, which means "four sides," and triangle, which means "three angles." A more consistent name for quadrilaterals that is also used is tetragon. A three-sided polygon can be called a trigon as part of the name trigonometry, which means "triangle measurement." Deca- (10), hendeca- (11), and dodeca- (12) are also Greek prefixes. These Greek prefixes are used to form the names decagon, hendecagon, and dodecagon.

After having observed geometric properties for figures (such as triangles and hexagons) enclosed by line segments that are joined together, one will discover that curved geometric figures also have interesting properties and many practical applications.

CURVES AND CIRCLES

Geometry includes the study of many kinds of curves. The kind that gets the most attention is the circle. It is a set of points that are all a certain distance, the radius, from a certain point, the center.

An interesting variation is to draw one point, draw a line, and do such things as finding all other points that are equidistant from that given point and that given line. Those other points would result in the black curve in the diagram in the page 32 diagram. That black curve is called a parabola. If one chooses to consider points that are, say twice as far from the point as from the line, then different curves may result.

DIRECTRIX, FOCUS, AND ECCENTRICITY

This technique is important enough so that special names are used for the line, the point, and

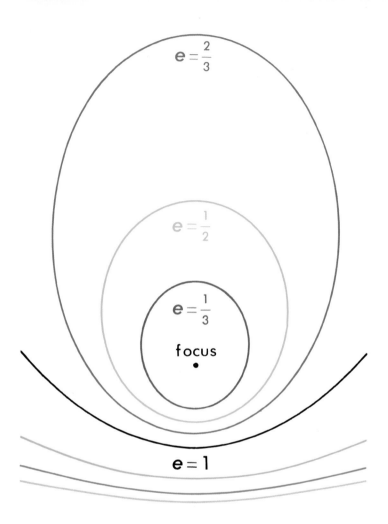

$$e = \frac{2}{3}$$

$$e = \frac{1}{2}$$

$$e = \frac{1}{3}$$

focus
•

$$e = 1$$

directrix

$$e = 4$$

$$e = 3$$

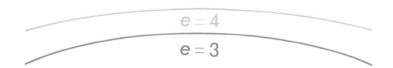

Different ratios between the distance to the focus (a point) and the distance to the directrix (a line) produce different curves. When this ratio—known as the eccentricity, or e—is between 0 and 1, an ellipse is produced. When e = 1, a parabola is formed, and when e is greater than 1, a hyperbola, with two separate parts, results. Encyclopædia Britannica, Inc.

the relation between distances. The drawn line is the directrix (plural: directrixes or directrices). The point is the focus (plural: focuses or foci). The ratio of distance-from-focus to distance-from-directrix is the eccentricity, or e.

Although further math involved is beyond the scope of what will be covered here, the eccentricity ratio, *e*, yields different graphs depending on its value. As the eccentricity takes values such as 1/3, 1/2, and 2/3, as shown in the diagram, each resulting ellipse stretches to look less like a circle and more like a football or an egg. As the eccentricity grows even larger, to a value of 1, the circle breaks apart below to become a parabola. When eccentricity grows to 2, 3, or 4, the result will be the hyperbolas shown below the parabola. (Each hyperbola has two branches, one above and one below the directrix.) One might say that a circle is perfect, but the more eccentric it gets, the more radically it changes from its original shape.

Each of these curved shapes has properties with enormous value in the world today. Detection systems to locate ships lost at sea rely on the hyperbola. Satellite dish television reception requires the parabola. Medical uses, as stated in the introduction, may require the ellipse. Many more applications exist.

These curves, a circle, an ellipse, a parabola, and a hyperbola can also be found by slicing

"THE GREAT GEOMETER"

Apollonius of Perga (262?–190 BCE) was affectionately called "The Great Geometer" by his friends because of his many accomplishments in the field of geometry. Specifically, it was his theory of conic sections, elaborated in his major work, *Conics*, that earned Apollonius the plaudits of his contemporaries.

A solid cone can be cut into sections, producing several unusual forms. Apollonius examined these conic sections, noted their shapes, and introduced the terms "ellipse," "hyperbola," and "parabola"

A Roman conical sundial from the 3rd century CE shows Apollonius's advanc[e] in depicting time. Incised in the surface of the conic section are the hour lin[es] and arcs that represent the winter solstice (top), the equinoxes (middle), and t[he] summer solstice (bottom). De Agostini Picture Library/Getty Images

to describe them. He was the first to recognize that these three forms, along with the circle, are all part of any cone. His *Conics* brought order to a confused and ill-defined area of geometry. His theory of conic sections is immensely useful to engineers, mathematicians, and everyday citizens.

Born in Perga, an ancient Greek town that lies in present-day Turkey, Apollonius studied in Alexandria, Egypt, and later taught at the university there. He traveled to several libraries and universities to expand his understanding of mathematics. In his numerous books (most of which have been lost), Apollonius acknowledged those who had studied the field before him, summarized their work, and proceeded to make his own contribution.

up a cone. For this reason these curved graphs are also called conic sections.

CONIC SECTIONS

The ellipse, parabola, and hyperbola—and sometimes the circle—are called conic sections because they are exactly the shapes formed by the intersection of a plane with a conical surface. Apollonius of Perga (262?–190 BCE) gave the conic sections—ellipse, parabola, and hyperbola—their names. He was the first to define the two branches of the hyperbola. His eight-volume treatise on the conic sections, *Conics*, is considered one of the greatest scientific works from the ancient world.

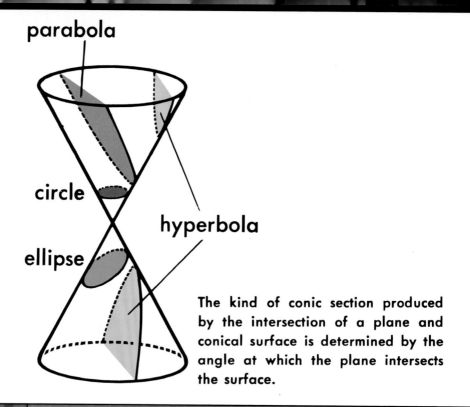

parabola

circle

ellipse

hyperbola

The kind of conic section produced by the intersection of a plane and conical surface is determined by the angle at which the plane intersects the surface.

The conic sections are produced by the intersection of a plane and a right circular cone (the surface traced by a moving straight line that always passes through a fixed point). Depending on the angle of the plane relative to the cone, a circle, an ellipse, a parabola, or a hyperbola is produced. Encyclopædia Britannica, Inc.

Circles, squares, triangles, parallelograms, and a variety of polygons, are two-dimensional shapes—they lie in a plane and do not occupy space (in other words, they have length and width but not depth). As students will observe in the next chapter, three-dimensional objects, called solids, have length, width, and height (or depth).

SOLIDS

S olid geometry deals with three-dimensional figures, such as spheres and cones. These figures have curved surfaces. A solid with only plane surfaces, however, is a polyhedron (plural: polyhedrons or polyhedra), such as a cube. Like polygons, polyhedra can be named by using Greek numeral prefixes. A tetrahedron has four triangular faces (see page 38).

PENTAHEDRA

A pentahedron, with five faces, can also be a pyramid, but with any kind of quadrilateral as its base. There are several other kinds of pentahedra (see page 38). Each of them has two triangular faces at opposite ends, with three quadrilaterals in between. Each, therefore, has six vertices (points) and nine edges (line segments). If these are counted

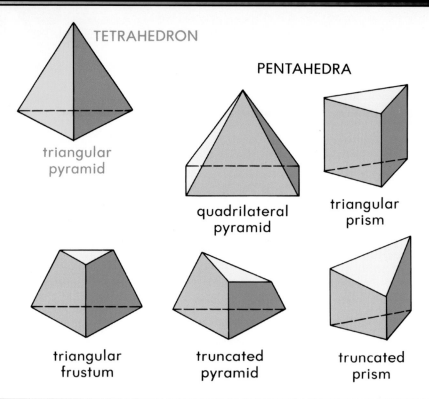

TETRAHEDRON

triangular
pyramid

PENTAHEDRA

quadrilateral
pyramid

triangular
prism

triangular
frustum

truncated
pyramid

truncated
prism

A polyhedron with four faces is called a tetrahedron. One with five faces is called a pentahedron (plural: pentahedra). Encyclopædia Britannica, Inc.

as variations of the same basic shape, there are only two kinds of pentahedra.

HEXAHEDRA

Even with such restrictions, there are 10 kinds of hexahedra, with six faces. Some of them have the same numbers of vertices and edges but in different arrangements. Each hexahedron can be distorted into variations that look different from one another. If, for example, one of the corners is cut off either of the pentahedra, making

HEXAHEDRA

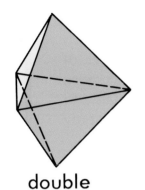

**double
tetrahedron**

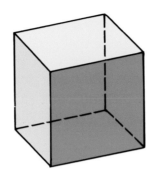

cube

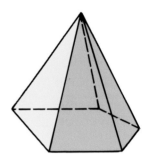

**pentagonal
pyramid**

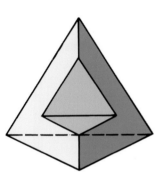
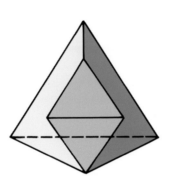
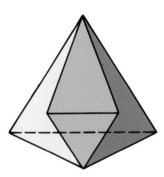

three kinds of notched tetrahedra

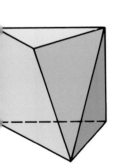
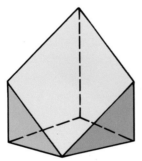
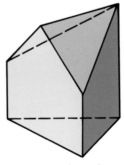
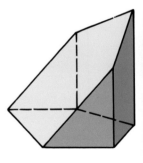

miscellaneous hexahedra

here are 10 types of hexahedra, each of which has six faces.
ncyclopædia Britannica, Inc.

ARCHIMEDES

The first scientist to recognize and use the power of the lever was Archimedes (287–212 BCE), who was born in Syracuse, Sicily. This gifted Greek mathematician and inventor once said, "Give me a place to stand and rest my

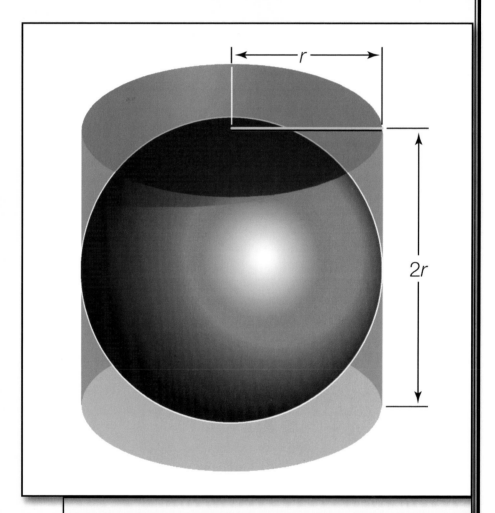

In his studies on a sphere with a circumscribing cylinder of the same height and diameter, Archimedes determined that any sphere has both two-thirds the volume and two-thirds the surface area of its circumscribing cylinder. Encyclopædia Britannica, Inc.

lever on, and I can move the Earth." He also invented the compound pulley and Archimedes' screw. Archimedes was a brilliant mathematician who helped develop the science of geometry. He discovered the relation between the surface area and volume of a sphere and those of its circumscribing cylinder.

A legend says that Archimedes discovered the principle of displacement while stepping into a full bath. He realized that the water that ran over equaled in volume the submerged part of his body. Through further experiments, he deduced the principle of buoyancy, which is called Archimedes' principle. According to this principle a body immersed in a fluid loses as much in weight as the weight of an equal volume of the fluid.

Another legend describes how Archimedes uncovered a fraud against King Hieron II of Syracuse using his principle of buoyancy. The king suspected that a solid gold crown he ordered was partly made of silver. Archimedes first took two equal weights of gold and silver and compared their weights when immersed in water. Next he compared the weights of the crown and a pure silver crown of identical dimensions when each was immersed in water. The difference between these two comparisons revealed that the crown was not solid gold.

a new face there, it may appear that a new kind of hexahedron has been discovered that is not among the 10, even though it is. Every hexahedron has four more edges than it has vertices.

The great variety among the hexahedra shows that it is not enough to name a solid by its number of faces alone. Figures are classified according to other properties, as suggested by the names of the pentahedra. Two important sets of polyhedra are prisms and pyramids, either of which may use any kind of polygons as bases. A pyramid with its top cut off parallel to the base becomes a frustum of a pyramid. Either a prism or a pyramid can have its top cut off not parallel to the base, forming new kinds of polyhedra—truncated prisms or truncated pyramids (see page 38).

REGULAR POLYHEDRA

Only five kinds of polyhedra are worthy of the name regular. Three of them have equilateral triangles as their faces; one has squares; and the other, regular pentagons. The double tetrahedron—one tetrahedron on top of another—shown among the hexahedra on page 39, almost qualifies, but it has two different kinds of corners. The five regular polyhedra are known as Platonic bodies because the Greek philosopher Plato investigated them about a hundred years before Euclid's time. The Greek mathematician Archimedes, who lived about the same time as Euclid, extended the investigation to solids that are almost regular and found them closely related to the regular ones.

While Euclid and his rules got geometry off and running, other mathematicians eventually followed with their own geometric ideas, and some of them suggested different, or non-Euclidean, rules. These conflicting views were not always easily accepted by the mathematics community, but over the years mathematicians began to find much value in them.

NON-EUCLIDEAN GEOMETRY

Euclid's fifth postulate asserts that, given a line and a point not on the line, there exists a unique line through the point and parallel to the given line. This postulate never seemed completely obvious, and mathematicians strove for centuries to find a proof for it based on Euclid's other, more obviously true, postulates. With no such direct proof forthcoming, some mathematicians began by assuming a different fifth postulate—either that there are infinitely many parallel lines (hyperbolic geometry) or that there are no parallel lines (elliptic geometry)—in the hopes of discovering a logical contradiction that would thereby indirectly prove Euclid's fifth. A particularly famous example of this was a flawed proof in 1733 by the Italian Girolamo Saccheri, based on the quadrilateral figure of the Persian Omar Khayyam (from about the year 1000).

HYPERBOLIC, ELLIPTIC, AND FRACTAL GEOMETRIES

There was no further progress until the Russian mathematician Nikolay Lobachevsky published the first paper on hyperbolic geometry in 1829. Although Lobachevsky continued his research in "imaginary geometry" for more than a decade, his work was not widely known or respected. It had little impact before the German Bernhard Riemann developed an axiomatic system for elliptic geometry in the 1850s. Riemann argued that the fundamental ingredients for geometry are a space of points (called today a manifold) and a way of measuring distances along curves in the space. He argued that the space need not

Bernhard Riemann is seen here in a lithograph that was based on a portrait, 1863. Archiv für Kunst und Geschichte, Berlin

be ordinary Euclidean space and that it could have any dimension (he even contemplated spaces of infinite dimension). Nor is it necessary that the surface be drawn in its entirety in three-dimensional space. Suddenly there were three incompatible geometries and a loss of certainty in geometry as the realm of indisputable knowledge. In 1871 the German Felix Klein compounded the problem by showing that all of these alternate geometries were internally consistent, leaving open the question of which one corresponds with reality. Near the beginning of the 20th century, Albert Einstein incorporated Riemann's work in his mathematical description of his theory of relativity (involving curved, or Riemannian, space). In the context of his general theory of relativity, Einstein showed that the true geometry of space is only approximately Euclidean. It is a form of Riemannian geometry in which space and time are linked in a four-dimensional manifold, and it is the curvature at each point that is responsible for the gravitational "force" at that point.

Benoit Mandelbrot's fractal geometry is used to describe irregularly shaped objects or natural phenomena—such as coastlines, snowflakes, and tree branches—that could not be described by Euclidean geometry. Mandelbrot coined the word "fractal" to signify certain complex geometric shapes. The word is derived from the Latin *fractus*, meaning "fragmented" or "broken" and refers to the fact that these objects

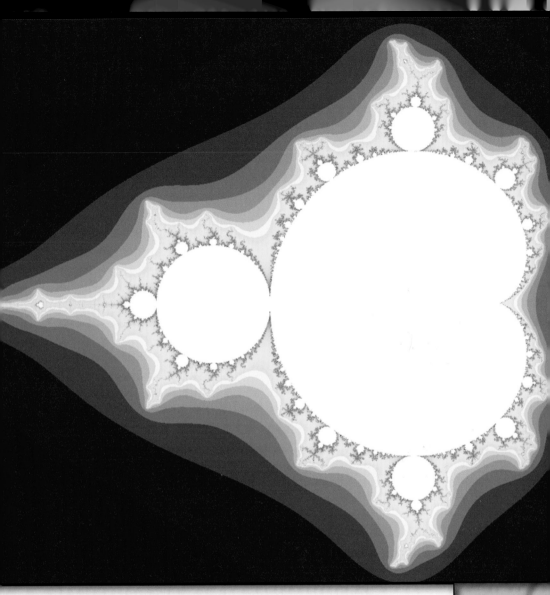

A Mandelbrot set, or fractal, an infinitely complex set of numbers, can be analyzed only with computers. Encyclopædia Britannica, Inc.

are self-similar—that is, their component parts resemble the whole. He stated that natural forms have the tendency to repeat themselves on an ever-smaller scale, so that if each component is magnified it will look basically like

BENOIT MANDELBROT

Universally known as the father of fractals, Benoit Mandelbrot (1924–2010) discovered a whole new branch of non–Euclidean mathematics. His discovery of fractals is used to describe diverse behavior in economics, finance, the stock market, astronomy, nature, and computer science.

Unlike mathematicians looking for nice and tidy order in the world of mathematics, Mandlebrot claimed he was always intrigued with the messy parts of math, the rough edges. In his memoir, *The Fractalist*, published in 2012, two years after his death, Mandlebrot wrote that his work on fractals was influenced by his interest in maps as a child. He thought about making "random coastlines from a simple formula." His discovery of his Mandlebrot set began with a simple quadratic equation into which he substituted a value, got an answer, and then plugged that answer back into the same equation. Then he iterated, or did the same thing again and again, thousands and thousands of times. Of course a computer did his calculations and plotted the values on a graph. He was surprised at the resulting graph he found. Small regions in the set look like smaller–scale copies of the whole set (a property called self–similarity). Mandelbrot's innovative work with computer graphics stimulated a whole new use of computers in mathematics. His colorful Mandlebrot set may be easily found and explored on the Internet.

His work is an example of modern discoveries in mathematics and is currently still evolving. Fractals are under intense mathematical study today.

the object as a whole. This geometry has been applied to the fields of physiology, chemistry, and mechanics.

SPHERICAL GEOMETRIES

The roots of elliptic geometry go back to antiquity in the form of spherical geometry. In spherical geometry everything resides on the surface of a sphere, making spherical geometry

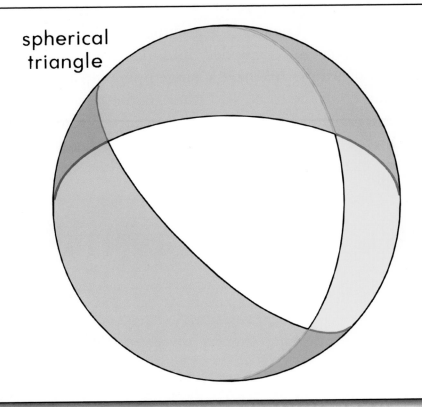

spherical triangle

In a spherical triangle, the angles add up to more than 180°. Encyclopædia Britannica, Inc.

central for cartography and astronomy. "Lines" are defined as the great circles—circles whose centers coincide with the sphere's center, dividing it into hemispheres. Great circles can form angles and triangles and other polygons. They can, in fact, do anything that lines do on a plane except be parallel. Any two great circles meet each other at two diametrically opposite points. Small circles (for example, the lines of latitude on Earth above and below the equator) can be parallel, but they do not have the other properties of straight lines.

From Euclid's beginning principles, geometry has exploded into discovery and applications that have changed people's lives and continue to do so. Other geometries that are non-Euclidean are emerging and continue to be studied to help advance humans' understanding of their world.

TRIGONOMETRIC FUNCTIONS

The building of the Egyptian pyramids may seem to have little in common with devising modern radar and H-bombs. But certain principles of mathematics enter into all such activities because they are fundamentals of the physical universe. Many are used in the division of mathematics called trigonometry. Many facets of trigonometry are beyond the scope of exploration in this book, but readers may glimpse one particular application (see Figure 1 on page 52).

The name "trigonometry" is from Greek words *trigonon*, meaning "triangle," and *metron*, "a measure."

Trigonometry deals with angle measure. Although angles are found in all triangles, angle measure is also important when viewed in many other ways. In the diagram on page 52, notice that as the angle θ grows larger,

Figure 1

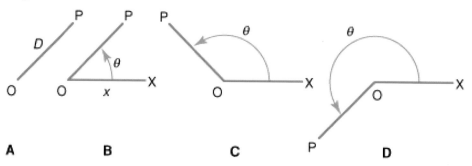

A B C D

segment OP swings around. But eventually OP swings back to exactly where it was. Every time it does, mathematicians say OP has gone through a cycle. This is called periodic motion because after one period is over, the next period (or cycle) begins. Even though the angle θ continues to grow larger, OP just repeats its cycle, similar to what happens when someone pedals a bicycle.

TRIANGLE MEASURE FOR CIRCULAR MOTION

Figure 2 (see page 53) shows another way that angle measure can describe periodic motion. Notice that the angle θ grows larger in diagrams A, B, C, and D. Notice that the length of line segment *y* at first would start at 0 length, grow larger (in diagram A) up to a value of 1, but

Figure 2

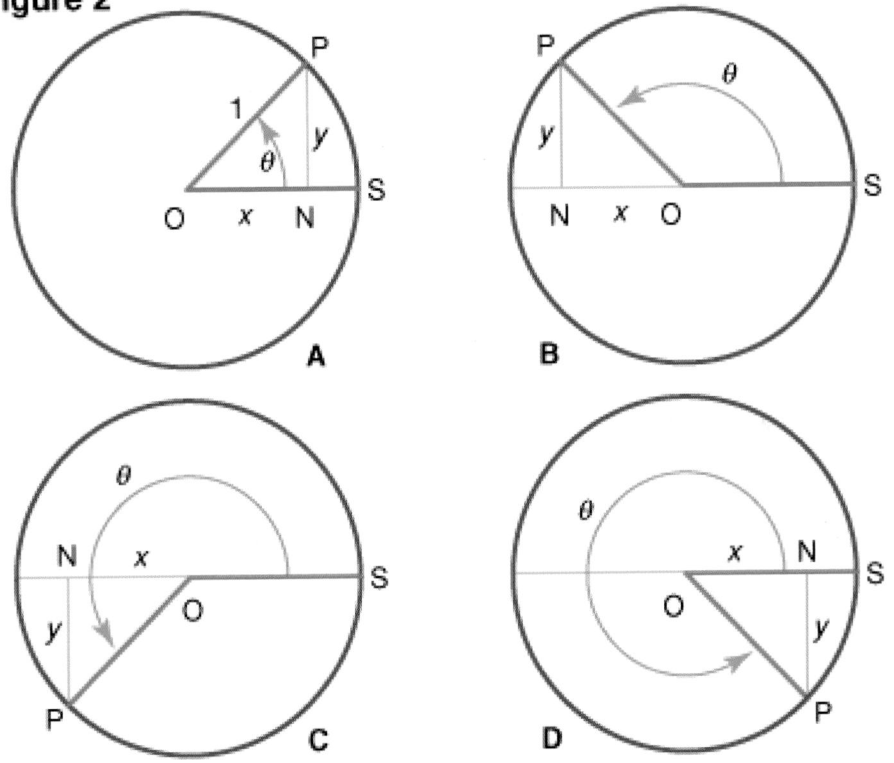

then smaller and smaller and back to 0 length in diagram B. Then y again grows to 1 in diagram C and then back to 0 in D. This is another example of periodic motion, y gets larger up to 1, then smaller back to 0, but always follows the same pattern, and then begins all over again.

Greek astronomer Hipparchus used the idea of periodic motion to make important astronomical discoveries.

HIPPARCHUS

Each day Earth goes through a period as it rotates completely around the sun and begins another period the next day: morning, night, morning, night, and so forth. A prolific and talented Greek astronomer, Hipparchus made fundamental contributions to the advancement of periodic astronomy as a mathematical science. He also helped to lay the foundations of trigonometry.

Born in Nicaea, Bithynia (now Iznik, Turkey), Hipparchus lived in the 2nd century BCE. As a young man he compiled records of local weather patterns throughout the year. Most of his adult life, however, seems to have been spent carrying out astronomical observations.

Hipparchus, like most other scientists of his day, assumed that Earth was stationary at the center of the universe and that the sun, moon, planets, and stars revolved around Earth each day.

Every year the sun traces out a circular type path in a west-to-east direction relative to the stars. Hipparchus had good reasons for believing that the sun's path, known as the ecliptic, is a great circle—that is, that the plane of the ecliptic passes through Earth's center. He discovered a method to calculate the sun's orbit.

Hipparchus also tried to measure as precisely as possible the length of the tropical year—the period for the sun to complete one passage. He made observations and compared them with observations made in the 5th and 3rd centuries BCE. This study led him to an estimate of the tropical year that was only 6 minutes too long. He knew he was onto something.

Hipparchus made the discovery that the positions of certain stars had shifted from the earlier measures. He did not know it then, but he had discovered a wobble in Earth's axis that has a period of almost 26,000 years.

He also applied his calculations to movement of the moon. Using early trigonometry and knowing the approximate distance between two known places, he was able to calculate the moon's distance as roughly 63 times Earth's radius. (The actual value is about 60 times, which is pretty close, or a good approximation.)

MEANING OF THE TERM "SINE"

The length of the line y for any given value of θ in the graph below is called the sine (abbreviation: sin) of the angle θ. This fact is usually written as the equation $y = \sin \theta$. The points on the graph below (figure 3) show how the values

Figure 3

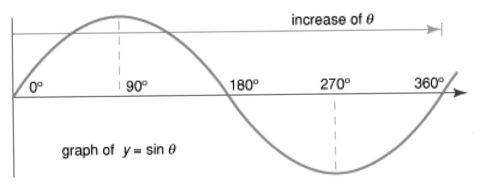

increase of θ

0°   90°   180°   270°   360°

graph of $y = \sin \theta$

of the y's are paired with the values of the θ's, for angles $\theta = 0°$ to $\theta = 360°$.

The graph is often called a sine wave for obvious reasons. The wave is even longer than it looks. As θ grows beyond $360°$ to the right, the curve repeats the cycle that is depicted in the graph. The cycles repeat out to infinity. Each cycle is a period. This curve shows periodic motion. It also is a visual representation of light waves, sound waves, and what individuals might see on a heart monitor screen in a hospital. When a musician tunes up his or her guitar, the sound waves come to people's ears in the form that is seen in this graph.

This trigonometry exploration with angle sizes and periodic motion presents only one view of coming attractions with trigonometry in mathematics. As students' backgrounds grow, more trigonometry principles will be presented in the high school and college years.

W hat readers have found in this book is that geometry and trigonometry principles hold important, broad, and varied appeal for them. The book also allows them to quickly get their hands on these principles when they need them, and those times will come whether they're taking a formal course of math or

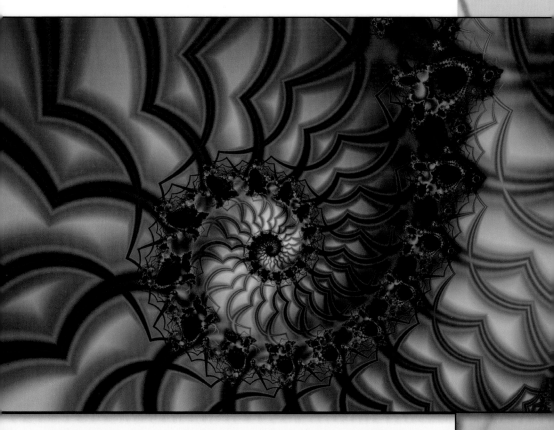

Many fractals possess the property of self-similarity. A self-similar object is one whose component parts resemble the whole. This repetition of details or patterns occurs at progressively smaller scales and can continue indefinitely, so that each part of each part, when magnified, will look basically like a fixed part of the whole object. © iStockphoto.com/lauchenauer

reading an online article. The exciting potential for further discovery is evident in the stories they've seen about the topics.

Some discoveries have practical uses that people might see right away, such as the gentle rise and fall of the sine curve, which is how alternating current voltage changes and also how the sound of a violin can be varied. And other discoveries might have simply an artistic calling for people, as in the story of Mandelbrot and his fractal geometry. One might even explore further, for instance, by tracking down the fascinating Mandelbrot set on any of dozens of Internet sites that allow everyone to create beautiful variations of this relatively new branch of fractal mathematics.

Math discoveries still await those who will find them. But to find them, the student might first browse again the pages of *Geometry and Trigonometry*, study the basics, and then let his or her mind wander.

algebraic Relating to a branch of mathematics that explores the relationships between numbers and the operations used to work with them and that uses letters or other symbols to represent them.

axiom A rule or principle widely accepted as obviously true and not needing to be proved.

breadth Distance from side to side, or width.

circumscribing Drawing a line around; constructing or having been constructed around (a geometrical figure) so as to touch as many points as possible.

conic section A curve formed by the intersection of a plane and a cone.

contemporaries People living at the same period of time.

drafter One who makes a draft of something, such as plans or designs of a building to be constructed.

eccentricity The amount by which a nearly circular path is not circular; in conics, it is the ratio of distance-from-focus to distance-from-directrix.

ellipse A closed plane curve that is a conic section of oval shape; a closed curve that consists of all points whose distances from

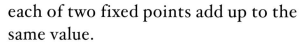

each of two fixed points add up to the same value.

equilateral Having all sides or faces equal.

Euclidean geometry The study of plane and solid figures based on the axioms of the Greek mathematician Euclid.

fractal Any of various extremely irregular curves or shapes for which any suitably chosen part is similar in shape to a given larger or smaller part when magnified or reduced to the same size.

hyperbola A two-branched open curve; a plane curve generated by a point so moving that the difference of the distances from two fixed points is a constant; a curve formed by the intersection of a double right circular cone with a plane that cuts both halves of the cone.

isosceles Being a triangle with two equal sides; being a trapezoid whose two nonparallel sides are equal.

non-Euclidean geometry Any geometry that is not the same as Euclidean geometry, such as hyperbolic geometry and spherical geometry.

parallelogram A four-sided figure whose opposite sides are parallel and equal.

periodic Repeating or cyclic; consisting of or containing a series of repeated stages, processes, or digits.

plaudits Enthusiastic approval, usually used in the plural.

postulate A statement or claim assumed to be true especially as the basis of a process of reasoning.

predecessor One that precedes; for example, a person who has previously occupied a position or office to which another has succeeded.

rhombic Having the form of a rhombus, a parallelogram with all four sides of equal length and usually with no right angles.

theorem A formula, proposition, or statement especially in geometry that has been or is to be proved from other formulas or propositions; an idea accepted or proposed as a demonstrable truth.

trisecting Dividing into three equal parts.

truncated In a cone or pyramid, having the apex, or pointed end, replaced by a plane section and especially by one parallel to the base; having the edges or corners cut off by a line or plane.

θ The Greek letter theta, often used to represent angle measure.

$y = \sin \theta$ The length of the line y for any given value of θ is called the sine of the angle θ and is written as this trigonometric equation. The graph of the equation is periodic.

American Mathematical Society (AMS)
21 Charles Street
Providence, RI 02904
(401) 455-4100
Website: http://www.ams.org
This society provides programs for students in
the mathematical sciences, including a summer math camp, online materials for math
help, a list of local math clubs, an online
magazine *Plus* that features math-related
articles and puzzles, and math competitions.

Association for Women in Mathematics
(AWM)
11240 Waples Mill Road, Suite 200
Fairfax, VA 22030
(703) 934-0163
Website: http://www.awm-math.org
The AWM works to encourage women and
girls to study math and to pursue careers in
the mathematical sciences.

Canadian Mathematical Society (CMS)
Canada Math Camp
Department of Mathematics
University of Toronto
563 Spadina Crescent
Toronto, ON M5S 2J7

Canada
(416) 978-2011
Website: https://cms.math.ca/MathCamps
The CMS promotes education in mathematics
and offers summer math camps for students
who have an interest in mathematics and its
applications.

MathBits.com
Website: http://mathbits.com
E-mail: Roberts@MathBits.com
This educational site provides fun and challeng-
ing lessons and activities for high school math
students.

MATHCOUNTS Foundation
1420 King Street
Alexandria, VA 22314
(703) 299-9006
Website: http://mathcounts.org
The MATHCOUNTS Foundation is a non-
profit organization that encourages middle
school students to become involved in the
exciting world of math. It provides math
competitions, information about math
clubs, and Math Video Challenge, which
supports students in making their own vid-
eos to teach math.

Mathematical Association of America (MAA)
1529 18th Street NW
Washington, DC 20036-1358
(800) 331-1622
Website: http://www.maa.org
The MAA gives access to math periodicals,
   books, e-books, and more. It has a website
   (http://www.maa.org/programs/students) that
   lists programs for high school students, as
   well as information about math clubs, mathematics contests, and summer math camps.

Mathematical Staircase, Inc.
278 Bay Road
Hadley, MA 01035
Website: http://www.mathstaircase.org
This organization offers educational programs
   to assist high school and college students
   in learning math and applying it to their
   daily lives. It also provides a summer pro-
   gram called MathILy, which helps students
   improve problem-solving skills and explore
   math in new ways.

National Council of Teachers of Mathematics
   (NCTM)
1906 Association Drive
Reston, VA 20191-1502
(800) 235-7566

Website: http://www.nctm.org

The NCTM is an organization that supports teachers of mathematics. Its Illuminations web page (http://illuminations.nctm.org/Search.aspx?view=search&gr=6-8) lets students see what sorts of lesson plans and activities their teachers can share in the world of math.

Technology Student Association (TSA)
1914 Association Drive
Reston, VA 20191-1540
(888) 860-9000
Website: http://teams.tsaweb.org

TSA offers TEAMS (Tests of Engineering Aptitude, Mathematics, and Science), an annual competition for middle and high school students to help them explore their potential for engineering. TEAMS assists students in applying their math and science know-how in practical and innovative ways to solve everyday challenges in engineering.

Texas Instruments
Geometry
P.O. Box 660199
Dallas, TX 75266-0199
(800) 842-2737
Website: http://www.ti.com

This technology company provides a web page, called TI Math Nspired, that presents ideas on geometry applications that use technology. Check out http://education. ti.com/en/timathnspired/us/geometry to learn more about points, lines, and angles, triangles, right triangles and trigonometry, quadrilaterals and polygons, and circles.

WEBSITES

Because of the changing nature of Internet links, Rosen Publishing has developed an online list of websites related to the subject of this book. This site is updated regularly. Please use this link to access the list:

http://www.rosenlinks.com/TSOM/Geom

Abramson, Marcie. *Painless Math Word Problems*. 2nd ed. Hauppauge, NY: Barron's Educational Series, Inc., 2010.

Barrow, John D. *100 Essential Things You Didn't Know You Didn't Know: Math Explains Your World*. New York, NY: W.W. Norton, 2009.

Batterson, Jason. *Competition Math for Middle School* (Art of Problem Solving). North Charleston, SC: CreateSpace Independent Publishing Platform, 2009.

Canavan, Thomas, Jr. *Math Standards Workout: Computation Skills: 50 Math Super Puzzles*. New York, NY: Rosen Publishing, 2011.

Curley, Robert, ed. *The Britannica Guide to Geometry* (Math Explained). New York, NY: Britannica Educational Publishing and Rosen Educational Services, 2011.

8th Grade Math Review. New York, NY: Learning Express, 2009.

Enrichment Math, Grade 8. Greensboro, NC: Carson-Dellosa Publishing, 2011.

Finish Line Math Strands: Geometry. Elizabethtown, PA: Continental Press, 2008.

Friedman, Mel. *Geometry Workbook*. Piscataway, NJ: Research & Education Association, 2008.

Hosch, William L., ed. *The Britannica Guide to Algebra and Trigonometry* (Math Explained).

New York, NY: Britannica Educational
Publishing and Rosen Educational
Services, 2011.

Hyde, Arthur. *Understanding Middle School
Math: Cool Problems to Get Students
Thinking and Connecting*. Portsmouth, NH:
Heinemann, 2009.

Intro to Geometry Grades 7 + (The 100+ Series
Common Core Edition). Greensboro, NC:
Carson-Dellosa Publishing, 2014.

Katz, Brian P., and Michael Starbird. *Distilling
Ideas: An Introduction to Mathematical
Thinking*. Washington, DC: Mathematical
Association of America, 2013.

Kelley, W. Michael. *The Humongous Book of
Geometry Problems*. New York, NY: Penguin
Group, 2009.

McKellar, Danica. *Girls Get Curves: Geometry Takes
Shape*. New York, NY: Penguin Group, 2013.

Pickover, Clifford A. *The Math Book: From
Pythagoras to the 57th Dimension, 250 Milestones
in the History of Mathematics*. New York, NY:
Sterling, 2012.

Romanowicz, Zbigniew, and Bartholomew
Dyda. *100 Math Brainteasers Grade 7–10*. New
York, NY: Tom eMusic, 2012.